AGAINST ALL ODDS

TERRELL GREEN

GET IT DONE PUBLISHING

Against All Odds
Copyright © 2020 by Terrell Green

EBook ISBN: 978-1-952561-09-2
Trade Paperback ISBN: 978-1-952561-08-5

Cover design by Blair Caffey
Contributor Mia Francois
Published by
Get It Done Publishing
Stone Mountain, GA 30088
www.getitdonepublishing.com

To my mom, Lillian Wade, for giving birth to me and allowing me to tell her story along with mine. To my father, William Green, my sister Tramisha (Misha) Collins, and my best friend Marquis (Quis) Sutton, who lives through me. And to my fans, making you smile helped me to find my joy. Thank you for the endless support. I love you guys!

To respect the privacy of my family and those connected to me, most names have been changed or left anonymous.

AUTHOR'S NOTE

I believe we all have a story, and I want to share mine. There has been a lot I've experienced in my life. Both the good and the bad have made me into the man I am today. You probably haven't seen this man on social media, but my experiences have definitely inspired the content I produce. I want you to take a walk in my shoes as you read this book. For eight years, it's been a personal goal to publish my first book about my life. Growing up, I never considered the things I experienced would produce so many mental health issues. These experiences, along with my best friend, Marquis Sutton, inspired me to write *Against All Odds*. It is my hope that the stories I share in each chapter serve as a source of hope and inspiration for those who grew up like me and struggled with anxiety, PTSD, and depression. You know, Marquis and I always dreamed about telling our story once we made it. Writing this book has helped me grow as a person; it took a lot of courage to talk about some of the stories in each chapter. With that being said, I hope you enjoy reading it and get a better understanding of who I am. Perhaps reading my story may even inspire you to take a deeper look at your life and consider how important your story is and the different ways you can share it to help others.

CONTENTS

MAMA'S BOY

Growing up as a child, I remember wanting to stay with my mom. I felt like I needed her love more than anything in the world. All I ever wanted was to be loved by her, but she really couldn't give me the love I wished for because she suffered from drug addiction. At the time, I was too young to understand what was going on, and it left me lost as a little kid. Nonetheless, I yearned for her love and attention. I felt lifeless whenever I wasn't around her. In retrospect, I was very confused because no one told me the truth about her addiction. Feeling like things were being hidden from me caused me to be very observant and low key, which resulted in me having to learn a lot on my own. Although staying with my dad would've been a better living situation, I craved a mother-son relationship; I guess you can call me a "mama's boy." I grew up like many other black kids from my neighborhood. I didn't have a lot of clothes, but my mom always kept food on the table, thanks to food stamps.

My mom lived in East Palo Alto, California, and had to take care of her younger sisters at a very young age. My grandma got incarcerated for stabbing her neighbor because they slapped my mom while my grandma was at work. The neighbor had mistaken my mom for a kid playing ding-dong-ditch on her door, a prank kids play. When my grandma came home, my mom told her what happened, and they went to the neighbor's door together to confront her. My grandma knocked on the door, and when the neighbor answered, she asked if she slapped my mom. The neighbor responded, "Yes, I slapped the little bastard!" That is when they began to fight. As they were fighting, my grandma, who had a knife on her the whole time, stabbed the neighbor sixteen to seventeen times and had to do five years in prison for it. Meanwhile, she had just got out from serving two to three years on a drug charge right before that incident. My mother was eleven going on twelve when my grandma did time for the drug charge. It's safe to say my mother did not have a normal childhood either.

She had to do things like cook, get her sisters ready for school, and pay bills. I remember her telling me these stories and how it forced her to grow up fast. Maybe it was her growing up fast that also played a part in her getting on drugs at eighteen, introduced to them by a family member. My mom told me how she and the family member would snort powdered cocaine together. Unfortunately, as history would show, she never was able to kick that habit.

I never got the chance to meet my grandma; she passed away from lung cancer before I was born. My mom was only twenty-two. As for my grandpa, my mom's dad, he's still alive and doing well. I remember going to see him once, but aside from that, we hardly speak. Our relationship is whatever, but in my heart, I wish we were a little closer.

My mom had four boys, including me, and three girls. My dad had four boys, including me, and two girls. They shared two boys. I have six brothers and five sisters. My younger brothers are twins. The last time I saw them, they were a couple of months old. At that time, I was only three and naive to what was going on. Later, I realized they were in a foster home; it's been almost twenty-one years since. I used to ask my mom about them, and it seemed as if she didn't want to talk about it. Honestly, I think she had no idea where they could be.

One of my main goals in life was to find them and have a relationship with them. When I was a kid, I would have dreams of playing and running around with them outside like brothers do. I remember trying to look up their names on social media and found nothing.

My little sister got took from my mom too, but the difference is we got to see her and still do. She's beautiful, smart, and attends the same high school I graduated from. Luckily, her foster parent stayed in the same city as us, making it easy to stay in contact with her. Plus, her foster mom was cool.

When I was younger, not having my brothers and sisters around left me in a really confused place. As I got older, I realized what was going on and why things had to be the way they were. My relationship with my older brother, Terrance, who I shared the same mom and dad with, was cool. He used to pick on me a lot about being a mama's boy. He wanted me to be under him and always go places with him, but I wouldn't because I wanted to be under my mom. He would hate that and always made jokes about me. But as I look back at the stories he would tell me, they were actually kinda funny. One specific story was when we were staying in a motel. We were both jumping around from bed to bed. I tried to do what he was doing, and I jumped, slipped, fell, and broke my arm. My mother started panicking and yelling, asking people to call the ambulance. I guess you can say I failed at trying to be the cool little brother.

As for Terrance and me, my dad eventually ended up getting full custody of us. We stayed with my dad at my grandma's house, my dad's mom, until my dad was able to move us into a place of his own. One day, I was in the bedroom, and my dad and brother were in the living room watching TV. I snuck out the window and ran to my mom's house, who at the time was staying with one of my sisters, Misha. As I look back on it, it's crazy to think I did that as a kid.

My dad did a great job taking care of my brother and

me. There would be times my mom would go on "a mission," and my dad, Terrance, and I would be out all day looking for her. This would last until the money ran out. Every time she got money, she disappeared. However long it was for her money to be gone was how long we went without seeing or hearing from her. What's crazy about all of that is even though my mom had her struggles, it never changed my love for her; I still always wanted to be around her. Terrance knew what was going on, and he wanted no parts of my mom. We were complete opposites.

Eventually, I went from spending weekends with my mom to staying with her full-time. We lived with my older sister Misha, and her two kids, Deondre and Shawnte. Misha and my mom had more of a sister-sister relationship. My mom had her at fourteen, so I guess that played a part. Misha would fill in that mother role I wanted my mom to play since we were around each other so much. There would be times when my mom would be gone on a mission for a couple of days, and my sister would take care of me. We were so close; our birthdays are just two days apart. Misha was laid back, loving, goofy, and smart. I used to love it when she cooked her baked chicken. She loved listening to Bay Area music, and Mac Dre was her favorite rapper.

After a couple of years of staying with Misha, my mom got her own apartment on the Westside of Fresno in Summer Crest Apartments. Staying with other people and going from house to house was over. I was extremely happy. My mom made it happen and did what she had to do to get us our own roof over our heads. I also was able to have my own room for the first time in my life. It was about time to have my own space since I was a junior in high school.

My mom was just as excited as me since it had been years since she had an apartment of her own. This made me look at her as a superhero; I was still naive to the fact that she was on drugs. My dad and my brother used to joke about me staying with my mom. They would say things like, "You'll be back once you see how your mom really is." None of that mattered to me. I had my mind made up and was happy to be with her. I later found out they were telling the truth. As the saying goes, a hard head makes a soft ass.

2

IS THIS LOVE?

In the beginning, staying with my mom was a breeze! I felt like I finally got what I always wanted—to be with her and have that mother-son relationship. Growing up, I would see kids in the neighborhood getting good Christmas and birthday gifts. As a kid, I always wanted a Mongoose bike. I would give my mom a Christmas list, but she was never able to get me any of the things I wanted. The money she did receive from welfare was getting spent on her personal needs. All of this made me start to resent holidays, among other things. I remember watching TV shows like *The Fresh Prince of Bel-Air* and *The Cosby Show* and visualizing my mom and I having a relationship like the black moms on TV had with their kids.

Living with my mom exposed me to a lot of things. Although she did a hell of a job covering up her addiction, she still had hard days and couldn't hide it. Her main struggle was with pills; she would take Somas, also known as muscle relaxers. I remember bringing my friends over to play Madden on PS2. My mom came out of her room high on Somas. When she would use them, she could hardly function. Walking slowly down the hallway, I thought to myself, *"Man, I hope she doesn't start trippin'!"* She stood still in the kitchen, nodding off while leaning on the counter. I looked at my friends and then looked back over at my mom. I was so embarrassed! While they continued to play the game, I tried to carry her back to her room. I remember her being really heavy, but I didn't want to ask my friends for help and draw more attention to the situation. Those types of moments would piss me off, and unfortunately, it wouldn't be the last time something like that happened.

One day, I was outside playing football in the back of the apartment building with my friends. I went for a deep pass, and the ball was thrown over my head. As I ran to pick up the ball, I saw my mom by the playground moving slow. I continued to play with my friends, hoping no one noticed her. She was high off Somas again, this time, in public. It reminded me of the walking dead, not to mention, we stayed on the third floor! I thought to myself, *"How the hell am I gonna get her up these stairs?"* It took me about five minutes to get her up and into the house. Luckily, no one saw us. I was so heartbroken.

One morning, she was warming up some leftover spaghetti and asked me if she could use my blue flip phone. At the time, I didn't know she was off the Somas when I gave it to her. When I went into the kitchen to get some food, I saw my phone in the pot getting cooked right along with the spaghetti. I was furious; it was the first phone I ever had, and at the time, I had only had it for about three weeks. Now, looking back, I can laugh every time I think about it.

Despite all the things going on, I stayed with my mom. The love I had for her was unconditional. I wanted to be with her, and I always thought things would eventually turn around. Even though things were hectic at times, my mom's smile always brightened up my day. I just wasn't ready to give up on her.

I started playing sports just to get my mind off the things that were going on at home. In fact, that's when I started to get the most love I've ever felt. My track coach, Mr. Poindexter, was the closest thing to a mentor. He used to tell me how he played in the NBA, so I looked up to him even more. By the time I was in the eighth grade, I started to get in trouble in school a lot. I was a class clown. Me and my boy almost got expelled for jumping the new kid on campus. Instead of getting expelled, the school decided to let us stay at school until lunchtime. Every day at lunch, we had to go home for the rest of the year and miss our fourth and fifth-period classes. One of those periods was math, so we weren't able to get the math education we needed. It was either that or get expelled from school.

In hindsight, my behavior at school was based on how I was living at home. I wasn't happy; I had a lot of anger built up inside me and just needed love. My history teacher, Mr. Hill, told me if I didn't get my act together, I would end up in jail or dead. That stuck with me my whole eighth-grade year. I still use it as motivation today. I knew I had to get my shit together because I wanted to play sports in high school.

By the time I was in high school, I was getting fed up with the living situation with my mom. My friends had the latest shoes and clothes while I was still wearing clothes I had in junior high. My big sister Pooh would give me her hand-me-down shoes, but I got to a point where I wanted my own. Plus, my feet were getting bigger.

My mom had a boyfriend who we'll call Ben. At first, I wasn't happy with her talking to him because I felt he would hurt her. Plus, I didn't know him from a can of paint. But as time went by, I started to like him. He walked with a limp and always had a Black & Mild in his mouth. Ben worked at the neighborhood store, and when he would get off, he would bring us snacks; he also helped my mom with her bills. Ben would drop me off and pick me up from football practice too.

He used to give me fifty dollars to buy shoes from one of his friends who sold Jordans out of the back of his trunk. One day, I went to school, thinking I was fresh. I had on a white T-shirt, blue jeans, and a pair of Jordans I bought from Ben's friend. One of my friends told me my Jordan logo had a butt, and they were fake. He showed me the difference between the logos. Sad to say, I got finessed. I had already purchased a few pairs from him. I never bought another pair from him again.

Money was tight, so I started to depend on girls to buy me things I couldn't get on my own. I learned that everyone couldn't live like the Banks or the Huxtables. Looking back, I'm not ashamed of my living situation with my mom. As a kid, I was embarrassed, but I made the best out of it. Love comes in many forms. Growing up, I wanted my mom to love me the way I envisioned love. Instead, she loved me the best way she could, and tried her hardest to provide for me—I'm grateful for that.

3

MISHA

In my eighth-grade year, my big sister Misha moved to San Jose, California, with her kids Deondre and Shawnte. She was only out there for a year and a half and then moved back. I was beyond happy when she came back because we had a bond that couldn't be broken.

When I was younger, my sister's first baby's father, Shawnte's dad, was murdered. He was at a friend's house, hanging out and having a good time when a car pulled up in the alley. He thought it was someone he knew, so he began to walk up to the car. When he got close, a guy rolled the window down and shot him in his head. My sister found out she was two months pregnant with my niece when it happened. This incident left her scared to do things around the house by herself. Even simple things like taking showers were tough for her. She used to make me stay in the bathroom with her until she got done so she wouldn't be alone; I was in kindergarten then.

My niece and nephew are more like my little brother and sister; that's how much they were around me. My sister would pay my mom to babysit the kids while she went out with her friends. One night, my sister went out to have a good time and didn't make it home.

It was a Friday night, and I had just come home from my JV football game. After I got settled in, I laid down on my bed. Misha came over to my mom's to drop the kids off. Before she left, she came into my room and started tickling me while I was falling asleep. Her breath smelled like she had been drinking Olde E, her favorite beer to drink on the weekends. She was in a playful mood—we laughed, joked around, and then she left to go out. I never thought in a million years that would be the last time I'd see her. It was around twelve or one in the morning when my mom got the call saying Misha had been shot. She was at a house party, and some dudes started arguing. Some of the guys left then came back to the party and started shooting. My sister was shot in the chest.

Terrance came into my room, woke me up, and told me what happened. I got out of bed and walked into the living room to see my niece and nephew crying their eyes out. They were only nine and ten at the time. I hugged my niece Shawnte, with little to say. I looked over to my nephew, Deondre, and he also had tears flowing down his face. My mom was at the hospital with some family and friends. Terrance, the kids, and I stayed at home waiting on the update from my mom. This ended up being the first time I ever prayed to God. I asked him not to take my sister away from the kids. The next morning my brother told me she didn't make it. My heart dropped, and another first happened to me, I questioned God. *Why?* Why did you have to take her from the kids? She had such a beautiful soul; I felt like God didn't take heed to my prayer. I felt lost, and I didn't understand why. Tramisha Collins, also known as Misha, died on Saturday, October 3, 2009. She was with my other big sister Pooh, Pooh's boyfriend, and my big cousin Meeka, who also got shot in the chest, but survived. My sister Pooh's boyfriend got shot too, and he didn't make it either. They were all innocent bystanders.

Her funeral was the first funeral I ever attended. I can still remember kissing her on the forehead while she laid in the casket. She was cold. At that moment, I realized how short life was. Although I was hurting inside, I didn't shed a tear for some reason, but it was by far the worst pain I felt in my life. It felt like a bad dream. I had never lost someone so close to me. I was still a quiet kid who didn't show a lot of emotion, so I decided to get a teardrop tattooed on my face to express how hurt I was. I went to the tattoo shop alone in downtown Fresno. I don't know how I was able to get the tattoo without an ID, but I got it. The whole time I was in the chair, I was thinking about my sister, Misha.

My classmates were confused by the tattoo. I was a good kid in high school with a promising future in sports with a teardrop tattoo on my face. Teardrop tattoos typically symbolize you killed someone. People were coming up to me at school saying things like, "Man, why you get that tattoo? You didn't kill nobody." I didn't care; it meant something to me. The teardrop tattoo for me symbolized tears of sorrow and how I felt about my life at the time. I could also tell my mom didn't take Misha's death well either; she was numb inside. She would often lock herself in her room and just listen to music. I guess that was her way of mourning. My sister's killer was never found.

I learned that life is too short, and you need to enjoy your loved ones while they are still living. Everyone deals with pain differently. Getting a teardrop tattoo was a way I dealt with my pain at the time. My sister was in my life for a reason. Even though she was only here for a short time, I'm still learning more about what that reason is day by day. I think grieving is a life-long process. Like my tattoo, I don't think pain ever goes away; you just learn how to manage it better with time. She would want me to live my life and be happy, not sad. So that's how I'm going to continue her legacy and make sure her kids are good just like she did for me.

4

NEW BEGINNINGS

During my junior year in high school, I started making a name for myself around my neighborhood in sports. I played football and ran track. I was the fastest in my part of town.

In track, my events were the 100 and 200-meter dash. My fastest time in the 100-meter dash was 10.74, and the fastest time in the 200-meter dash was 21.74. I won all my events, which led me to the state meet. This gave me the opportunity to compete against big schools around California. People in my neighborhood would come knock on my door and have me race anyone they thought would be able to beat me.

In football, I was the starting slot receiver on the team. I caught 62 passes for 1,101 yards, which was the second-best in my high school history. I always felt like sports were going to be my way out. Mr. Poindexter was the first person that noticed my potential. He let me know I could do anything I put my mind to. That is what made me take sports seriously. The only thing I lacked was the academics. My mom didn't come to a lot of my games, I had to go home and tell her how many touchdowns I scored, or she would watch the highlights later that night on the eleven o'clock news. My dad, on the other hand, didn't miss a game.

The friends I hung out with in high school all had a little swag, but as I said in Chapter 2, my living situation with my mom made it hard to even get one hundred dollars for school shopping. I was still wearing clothes from middle school. That's when I started to rely on my girlfriends for money and school clothes. I would then gamble my money playing Xbox with my friends after school, and that's how I kept a little money in my pocket. I used to put the money I won in my dresser under my clothes, but I would come home from school, and it would be gone. I would ask my mom if she'd seen it. She'd say no and blame it on one of my cousins. I just shrugged it off and took my L's. It continued to happen, and I was getting fed up and upset, but it was what it was.

The only thing that kept me sane was sports. It took my mind to a different place. I used it as an escape route. I forgot about everything once I stepped foot on the football or track field. The feeling I got from scoring a touchdown or taking first in the 100-meter dash was better than any feeling I felt at home. It gave me hope, and I became optimistic about my future. I would fantasize about living in a big house with my family, my mom being off drugs, and just living comfortably without having to look over my shoulder. Despite what I was going through, I kept my head up and stayed positive.

At the start of my senior year, I felt like it was time for a change. My mama's boy days were over. I got tired of seeing my mom on drugs and even more tired of not seeing any changes. The last straw was seeing a piece of burnt foil rolled up like a blunt in my mom's bathroom. I had a talk with Terrance about what I had seen. He told me straight up it was a homemade crack pipe. My heart was broken again. I wanted to go somewhere where I could just focus on school and sports. Starting off my senior year, I realized I had to make something happen on my own. I decided to move in with my dad on the north-side of town.

When I moved in with my dad, it felt like a fresh start. He was laid back and chill just like me, so we would just vibe together. My dad had more structure than my mom and had no problem letting me know when I was messing up. That was the big difference between them. My mom let a lot of things slide. My dad was a different story; he would not let nothing slide. And I would hear his mouth about it all-night-long.

He helped me transfer my welfare case to his name so I'd be able to receive all of my money. By making this move, I was finally able to buy school clothes. I was getting about $200 to $300 monthly. All he wanted from me was to put food in the house with my food stamps, which seemed like a smooth deal for me. He put me up on game because I didn't know how the welfare process worked. He also taught me how to drive, so I would be able to get back and forth to school. Around this time, he couldn't get up every morning like he used to because he was getting really sick and couldn't be as active.

As I look back, it's crazy that I neglected a relationship with my dad because I wanted to be around my mom. But we made up for the time we didn't spend together as much as we could, and I don't think me staying with my mom affected our relationship. My dad knew I would come back around once I got old enough to know about my mom's addiction. We would stay up all night and talk about his childhood. One of my favorite stories he told was when he was a dancer with the Electric Boogaloos, a pop-lock dance crew. His name was Tickin Will. He said that famous entertainers would send scouts to watch them dance. Man, he had stories for days.

Although I moved in with my dad, I would still stop by my mom's house after school at times or even spend the night because she stayed closer to my high school. It felt like I overlooked the love my dad had for me, and that's one of the few regrets I carry now. I've learned that sometimes you miss what you need searching for what you want. No matter which direction you take, you'll end up in the right spot. But, it's up to you to press the reset button to a new beginning.

5

QUIS

In the fifth grade, I met Marquis Sutton. He reminded me of myself in so many ways. He was laid back, open-minded, and real. We ran track together, and that's how we developed a close bond. Our lives were very similar, as well. Both our moms had drug addictions, and he was in a foster home for some time in his childhood. Although I was never in foster care because I had siblings that were, I understood his pain. We lost contact for some years after he left West Fresno Elementary School. The next time we saw each other was my junior year in high school. He had transferred from Bullard High School, which was on the other side of town.

I was leaving the counselor's office, and I saw him in the registration office. He looked at me and said, "Terrell!" and I was like, "Quis?" We dapped each other up, and from there, our friendship picked up from where it left off. It felt like I found a long-lost friend. We would hang with each other all day at school, reminisce on our elementary school days at West Fresno, and eventually, I convinced him to join the track team. Marquis was somebody I could trust. He was like the little brother I've always wanted. Our bond was more than just friends; we looked at each other as family from jump.

My freshman year at Fresno City College had just begun, and my dad would let me drive his car to school. Marquis would spend the night with me, and I would take him to Edison High School in the morning before my classes started; he had one more year left. After school, I'd pick him up and take him to his mom's or girlfriend's house. Otherwise, he would stay the night at my dad's house with me. We would sit in my room and just talk about life. We always had deep conversations and would talk about God, death, the Illuminati, and our futures. We both said we wanted to write a book about our life to tell people about our testimony. It was crazy how much we connected.

September 25, 2012, a day I'll never ever forget. It felt like it was going to be another regular day. I had picked my nephew Deondre up from my mom's house, and then we went up to Edison to pick up Marquis from school. We barely had gas, but we made it home, luckily. Then, we got hungry, but we had no money either. So, Marquis decided to sell his iPod touch on Craigslist just so we would be able to have gas money to make it to school the next morning and buy a pizza for dinner that night. That act of kindness just showed how good of a person he was.

A guy contacted him, wanting to purchase the iPod touch. We agreed to meet at the store across the street from my dad's house. The guy let us know he was at the store, so Marquis, Deondre, and I walked across the street to meet him to make the sale. Marquis originally was selling the iPod touch for $80. When the buyer arrived, he said he only had sixty dollars, but he really wanted it for his son. Marquis being the good person he was, let him buy it for just $60. As the man and his son drove off, I told Marquis, "You're stupid bruh, you could've got your full $80 from someone else." He responded calmly, "It's alright bruh, God is gonna bless me." I thought about what he said, and I agreed with him.

At the time, Marquis was dealing with an ankle injury, so he had a limp. He was going to be the starting corner-back that year and had plans to attend San Diego State University. Once we got done, we began to head back across the street to my dad's house so we could order the pizza. Marquis knew his friend stayed in the apartments nearby and wanted to stop by his house, so my nephew and I went with him. When we got close to the door, his friend had a dog that ran our way. We all saw the dog coming, so we started to run. Marquis was laughing and running with a limp as he yelled and told his friend to get his dog. While he was laughing, the friend told his dog to stop.

We were at his friend's apartment for about thirty minutes. My nephew and I sat down in the kitchen while Marquis stood up by the front door, talking to his friend.

To respect everyone and their families involved, I won't go into detail on the full incident. What I will say is eventually, I heard a click sound; then, a second click and the gun went off. It happened so fast. I covered my ears with my eyes closed, with my nephew right by my side. Once I opened my eyes, the whole house was silent for about fifteen seconds. The first thing I did was looked up at the ceiling, hoping I'd see a bullet hole. As soon as I looked down, I saw Marquis laying down holding his neck gasping for air. He had been shot in his back, and the bullet traveled out of the side of his neck. At this point, I was in complete shock. It was my first time hearing a gunshot so close to my ear; my eardrums were ringing. All I could hear was how fast my heart was beating. My nephew cried out loud, "Marquis!" Someone yelled, "Call the paramedics." But at that point, I was in a different state of mind. I felt as if I was waiting for someone to wake me up, literally! It felt like a bad dream. I had my phone in my pocket, but I was too shocked to think straight.

We waited for the paramedics to arrive. While he was fighting for his life, I looked at Marquis, still in complete shock, I couldn't even speak. It felt as if I was in a nightmare. My nephew was crying as he tried to get a response from Marquis, but he didn't respond. Marquis was pronounced dead at the hospital later that night. The police took my nephew and me down to the police station for questioning.

They took Deondre back to answer some questions

first, then they called me back. When the detective asked me what happened, I refused to tell him anything. I didn't want to be labeled as a "snitch." The next couple of days, there were rumors going around that I had Marquis set up, or we were targeted by gang members. The story in the news media was a "Russian roulette-style death." They made it sound like we were all volunteering to play Russian roulette, which wasn't the case. It was all these different stories and rumors spreading about what had happened that night. The only people that knew what happened were the people closest to me; I just refused to tell the police.

After the incident, I felt like dying too. I started to question God for the second time, asking him why? Why him and not me? With the things I was going through in my head afterward, I wished I had got shot that night too. For so long, I wondered why this had to happen. Things didn't add up. I turned to God and started to attend church, but I just couldn't get into it, I felt nothing. I stopped going to football practice, and I didn't want to be around anyone. That situation made me more conscious of my surroundings, for sure. I stayed in the house and started smoking weed and taking pain pills to cope. I started to follow in my mom's tracks, and I became addicted to Narcos, Percocet, Codeine syrup, and sometimes Xanax. It made me numb. I was trying to run away from my past, inner demons, and toxic thoughts that crossed my mind daily. The pain I felt, I could never really explain. I had no one to talk to, and it was really depressing.

I stopped being around large crowds and was paranoid all the time. I opened the Bible and started reading. I needed something more to help me get through the hard times. I started to pray every day, asking God for understanding and wisdom to understand why things happened the way they did. Eventually, I started to see things through scriptures, which gave me hope. There would be times when my friends would come over, and I'd be excited to tell them about certain passages I had read. I can say a lot of people stopped hanging with me while I was in the midst of finding myself and trying to get a stronger connection with God. I was losing friends, and my family members thought I was losing my mind. I was headed on a spiritual path, and a lot of my friends weren't having it, but I really didn't care. I felt the presence of God everywhere I went for the first time.

I still think about that day. I even still have terrible dreams, like hearing a loud gunshot that leads me to jump out of my sleep. When it happened, I couldn't sleep to save my life. There were times I thought about saying fuck everything. I thought about hitting the streets and throwing my life away because I felt like I had nothing else to lose. It was very tempting, when everyone around you is in the streets, nine times out of ten you're going to fall into that life too. But no matter how hard times got, I stayed true to myself and stuck to the script because God had other plans for me.

Life is a big mystery. As cliché as it sounds, I truly believe God works in mysterious ways. Maybe it's not for me to focus on why things happen but how to move forward. The last thing Marquis told me was how God was going to bless him for doing a good deed. He died a couple of hours later. I don't have all the answers and still can't fully make sense to how that connects. But I do know that one decision can change your whole life, or worse, cost you it.

6

VIRAL!

After Marquis was killed, I moved from Fresno to Visalia, California, to attend a junior college out that way. I needed a fresh start. I made the football team and also still ran track, but it seemed like no matter what I did, I was hindered by my thoughts. I wasn't myself, and I couldn't shake it. I remember one day I was at football practice completely out of it. I was dropping balls, playing timid, I just couldn't get my head in the game. Track season was tough too. Before every race, I thought about the incident, and I was out. The trauma I was dealing with was unbearable. I felt so weak. Then I gave up on football. Shortly after, I dropped out of school and moved back with my dad. My family depended on me. We all had high hopes I would get us out the hood, and I didn't live up to it. I felt like a loser. I threw it all away. Everywhere I went, people asked me about football and wanted to know if I was still going to be playing. I'd tell them no because I didn't have love for the game anymore.

I found myself at my dad's not doing anything, just living with regrets and a heart full of sorrow. In a lot of ways, I felt like I was by myself with no one to confide in. I was still stuck in the past, and life was passing me by. My dad would try to persuade me to go back to school so I could get back in sports, but I had my mind made up—I was done. At that time, I wasn't receiving money because my welfare stopped. So, I had to look for a job to help my dad with the bills, but I couldn't find a place to hire me. I don't know if it was because of my neck and face tattoos or my lack of experience. Whatever it was, it didn't sit well with me, so I told myself I would figure out how to create and own my own shit.

One day, I was scrolling down my timeline on Facebook, and I saw a funny video clip that caught my attention. I was amazed at how creative the guy was. I started to think to myself, "Nigga, you always had people rolling in class; you should give it a shot." So, I jumped off the porch and made my first skit.

In the process of creating the video, I was amazed at how easy it came to me to edit the clips I put together. I grabbed a clip I saw on the Internet and just added myself to it as If I was actually there. I was nervous, and I didn't know what people were going to think. But I had nothing to lose, so I uploaded it. The feedback I received was crazy. Everyone on my friends' list was laughing and sharing the video. I even had friends I went to college with that were from different states share the video too. All the sharing kept my views growing. My cousin and I started making videos together, and people all over California were sharing them. That's when I knew I had something. I saw where I could take it, so I continued to make them every day.

For the first time in a long time, I was happy. I was able to make people laugh and brighten up their day. When people saw me in public, they'd tell me how funny my videos were instead of asking me about football. On New Year's Eve, going into 2014, I decided to stay home, and one of the things I did that night was talk to God. I remember telling him I wanted to go viral and take it to the next level. So, the next morning, I made a video from an idea I came up with. There was a viral video of a girl dancing crazy, so I thought it would be funny to act like we were on FaceTime together. After I posted the video, I took a shower, and once I got back to my phone, my Facebook and Instagram notifications were ringing off the hook! I went viral getting over two million views within twenty-four hours. I gained a fan base overnight from all over the world! I couldn't believe my eyes; people were saying they loved me and how I made their day. People from different countries would write and tell me how funny I was. I couldn't believe it; all I could do was thank God.

It felt like I won the lotto; I looked forward to each day, and I was motivated again. Although I was hurting inside from the deaths of Misha and Marquis, I was able to put a smile on millions of people's faces. That type of shit made me feel really fortunate and blessed.

I used to hear how people were getting paid off YouTube views, so I decided to make one and hoped the views I was getting on Facebook would translate to YouTube. It was a slow process, but I was able to gain thousands of subscribers rather quickly and received my first paycheck check from YouTube a couple of months after creating my channel. My first check was $500. That was a lot of money to me at that time, and it was the first check I ever received in my life. It amazed me how I could go from being down and out to making money doing something I loved. When it hit me, a nigga cried tears of joy. I remembered the hard times growing up, and that's why I remained humble through all my achievements. I was getting blessed from left to right.

I also made a promise to myself that I wasn't going to give up on myself this time. Honestly, being a social media comedian wasn't a dream of mine. I was having fun, but I was also trying to figure out how to cope with my own pain. That pain turned to me falling in love with my craft and making people laugh. There would be times when I would just sit in my room and cry because I knew God was preparing me to share my testimony with the world. I promised myself I wouldn't let the internet fame get to my head. Being humble is something that is important to me. I remind myself daily where I came from and the challenges I had to face in order to get where I am today. I remember the talks Marquis and I used to have about sharing our testimony. Like the time we talked about writing a book about our lives. I made a promise to him I was going to keep his name alive.

Going viral was one of the best things that happened to me. I would never have thought I would be an inspiration to people around the world. The fact that I'm able to inspire young men and women around the globe is mind-blowing. I learned we all go through trials and tribulations, but how you handle hard situations will determine your fate. Looking back, I don't know how I made it through, but I did, and so can you.

7

POPS

According to WRNB Philly, nearly 70% of African American children live in father-absent homes. Most of my friends grew up without their dad in their life. Luckily, I had my dad in my life, and we had a pretty good relationship. My dad was a strong guy, and he loved his kids. I hope I'm half the man he was.

He was on dialysis for almost his whole life. He was beaten up by the police badly. As a result, he had kidney failure and other major health problems. Back then, police brutality was just as bad, if not worse than it is today. Unfortunately, that was a normal thing for black people around my way. He ended up winning a lawsuit against them. I never knew how much he won, but anytime I asked him about it, he would just always say it wasn't enough.

When I was in middle school, his leg got amputated along with a few fingers. He didn't let that steal his joy, though. He stayed moving around and reminding my brothers and me about his dance moves. He would tell me stories about how he traveled to different cities and states for performances before he got sick. As I got older, my dad got sicker, but somehow, he still was able to make it to all my football games and track meets. Seeing my dad at my games in the condition he was in meant the world to me. He continued to show love and support no matter what. It gave me life when I would look up and see my dad in his wheelchair, supporting me. After I graduated from high school, things started to change. I had to take care of him and help him get around the house. Sometimes I would stay in the house all day to make sure he was okay. But I also wanted to go out and have fun with my friends. I felt bad because I would be out having fun while my dad was at home needing my help.

One specific night I was at a party with my boys. When I got home, my dad told me he had fallen off the bed. I was upset at myself for not being there. But I was a young man, so my dad had no problem with me going out as long as I made it back before he went to dialysis. I admired his strength and independence because he was so determined and wanted to get things done regardless of his condition.

One of the most terrifying moments I had with my dad was when I had to call the paramedics because blood was gushing out of his arm. He would have random health scares like this at times. I was in my room lying down when I heard him yell for me. I ran into the living room to see what he wanted, and that's when I saw him holding his arm trying to stop the blood from gushing. I grabbed a towel so I could put pressure on the area the blood was coming out from. The blood was coming out so fast it left a puddle on the couch, and the towel I had was completely covered in blood as well. I called the paramedics, but it took them literally forty-five minutes to come. I was scared I was going to lose him. I think we were both shocked he survived with the amount of blood he lost.

Those days were tough—he stayed in and out of the hospital. Every time he came home, though, he would go back to his usual self, being in good spirits and cracking jokes. I definitely got my humor from him. No matter how bad it got for him, he always would try to make you laugh.

As time went by, I decided to move out and stay with my girlfriend. My dad and I had a disagreement over money. I wanted to be his care provider since I was staying with him and was doing the majority of the work, but he kept it in one of my brother's name, who hardly came over. That pissed me off, so I moved out. I stayed down the street from him, so I would still go over and help him if he needed me.

A couple of months went by, and I got a call that my dad was in the hospital. I went to visit him, and he seemed fine. I thought to myself, "Oh, he'll be okay like always," but that wasn't the case. In fact, it was his last trip to the hospital. I got a call saying it wasn't looking too good, so I rushed to the hospital. When I entered his room, I saw him lying on the bed, taking his last breaths. I looked him in the eyes. He couldn't speak, but it felt as if he was trying to tell me something. I grabbed his hand and said a prayer while crying. For the second time in my life, I had to look someone I loved in their eyes as their life slowly faded away. I got home and cried myself to sleep. The next morning, March 14, 2016, my dad passed away.

I felt guilty because I was supposed to be with him. It bothers me that I walked out on my dad while he was sick. Although my dad passed away, I know he is in a much better place. He doesn't have to suffer anymore—no more dialysis, no more aches and pain; he can dance in heaven with God. I still grieve over my dad's death, but at the same time, I know God had prepared me for it by allowing me to see Marquis get killed and feel the pain of losing Misha. He gave me the strength I needed to keep pushing and chase my dreams.

I learned that not everyone is lucky to have their father in their lives. As I look back, I am grateful for the time I had with my dad. Although he isn't here to see me prosper, I will continue to make him proud and keep his name alive.

8

BLOOD BROTHERS

I used to go to sleep at night, praying to meet my younger twin brothers. I would sometimes visualize meeting them. The picture I painted in my head felt so real; I just knew one day it was going to happen. There were rumors my dad called CPS on my mom the day she had them because he was jealous she moved on and had kids by someone else. I never asked my dad about it because I didn't know how true that rumor was. Then there were also rumors that it was another family member. One of my cousins confirmed it was, in fact, that family member who made the call. I was so hurt and disappointed after finding out. I don't know exactly why they did it. Whatever their reason was, I don't think it was cool. They broke up a family. I found out the truth after my dad passed away. My dad had a good heart, and it sucked he passed away with people assuming the worst about him.

I stated back in Chapter 1 that one of my goals in life was to find my twin brothers. We found them Saturday, March 23, 2019. I was in the middle of editing a video when I got a phone call from one of my nieces. She told me they found the twins. I was stuck; I didn't believe it. The first thing I said was, "You sure it's them?" When we got off the phone, I instantly thanked God for answering my prayers.

She sent me a screenshot of one of their Facebook pages, so I decided to message him. Twin1 was just as excited as I was to talk to each other. He told me he always wanted to meet his real family. I asked him where Twin2 was, and he replied, "With friends." My mom wanted to meet them as well. It would be the first time she would see them since they were babies. I talked to her before the meeting. She was nervous but also excited; it had been twenty-plus years.

A week later, all my mom's kids were supposed to meet up at her house—the night before I couldn't sleep. I had so much anxiety and excitement running through my mind on my way there, my hands were sweating, and I had butterflies in my stomach. All I could do in the car ride was think about all my daydreams of that moment. When I arrived at my mom's house, the first person I saw when I opened the door was Twin1. He had a big Kool-Aid smile. We approached each other at the same time, dapped each other up, and hugged. It was a huge sigh of relief. I asked him where Twin2 was, and he said he was anti-social and didn't like big crowds. It sucked we couldn't meet both of them the same day, but I under-stood. I met Twin2 two weeks later at a bar in Kingsburg, California, where they both lived. It was a warm welcome when I met him. We talked, took shots, and all three of us took our first picture together.

My relationship with my brothers isn't what I would want it to be, but it's truly a blessing that I found them and can contact them any time. Their names were changed to Emmett and Seth—less black names to the ones they were given if you ask me. That's why it was so hard to find them all those years. Their foster parents were white, but a very nice family who nonetheless loved them unconditionally. Twin1 moved in with me after he got into a situation with his foster dad. We also made a few videos together.

He had questions on why things happened the way they did. He told me he grew up confused. He said he'd ask his foster mom why she was white, and he was black. He also told me his family was judged for adopting them. His pain was totally different from mine. He asked me a few questions about my childhood and how it was growing up with my mom. Some questions he asked, I couldn't give him any answers, but I told him what I did know. He was told my mom threw them away in a dump-ster. I told him that wasn't true, but I don't know if he believed me.

As for Twin2, we text from time to time. He hasn't met my mom yet, and I don't think he plans on doing so either. I think he believes my mom wanted nothing to do with them, so he has no intention to meet her. It's been a year since we found them; I hope he comes around. I'm the only person in the family who has met him. I understand his frustration, so all I can do is leave it up to God. My mom said she still plans on meeting him but is willing to give him as much time as he needs.

I learned that with faith, you could do just about anything. Looking back, I had faith I would find my brothers. Although it took longer than I expected, I'm grateful to have them in my life finally.

9

BLESSINGS

Despite all the losses I've taken, God keeps on blessing me. I signed my first major contract as a content creator in 2019. It felt unreal to get my first deal. All the hard work I put in over the years is paying off.

God has also placed some people in my life that I prayed for, needed really. I'm at a point where it's vital to have positive relationships. I'm starting to meet people like Richard Taylor Jr., my book coach and speaker/author, who himself has dealt with and overcome mental health problems. If it weren't for my big brother Blair and big sister Mia, this book would still be on hold in my iNotes. And really, outside of the book, they've all given me guidance and love I didn't know I needed.

It was hard to walk away from relationships with friends that were holding me back. I couldn't prosper if I was going to be hanging out smoking, drinking, and popping pills. It wasn't good for my mental health, and at this point, I can't afford to be around any negativity whatsoever.

I realized this journey I'm on is a marathon, not a sprint (RIP Nip). A lot of my friends were speeding through life instead of taking their time. One of my close friends was sentenced to thirty years in prison not too long ago. I would always tell him to slow down, but his way of normal was the only thing he knew. I was with him the day his mom passed away. It was tough. Imagining being with someone right after they get a call saying their mom has passed away. From that day on, he wasn't the same. It's like he had nothing left inside of him.

Being patient paid off for me. It helped me find my "why" for living. Doing the self-work is hard, but it will all be worth it in the long run. One of the key things I do now is meditate; it helps me with my anxiety and depression. I discovered it while on Google one day, looking up ways to help with PTSD and anxiety. After trying it a few times, it eventually turned into a habit.

Meditation also helps me manage my depression; I think of positive thoughts while I'm meditating. I also love listening to ocean sounds while meditating; it takes me to a peaceful place. I try to speak positive thoughts to myself as much as possible as a reminder I'm no longer living with guilt from my past. I realized if I think negative, then more likely negative things will continue to occur in my life.

I learned to forgive others; you can't get anywhere with hate in your heart. Today, I can say I'm no longer a prisoner of my guilt. It was all a toxic mental game I was subconsciously playing in my head. I was at war with myself. Now, I'm learning to love myself and others. I came a long way, but I still got so far to go—one day at a time.

My mom has been trying her best to be clean and sober. The fact that she's trying makes me happy. I want her to be around to see me win. I want to move her out of Fresno. I want her to see me do the things I promised her I would do. I already lost my dad; I'm not trying to lose her anytime soon.

I frequently thank God that I didn't lose my mind after seeing my best friend lose his life. Around that time, there were lingering thoughts of death roaming my mind. Now, I fight those thoughts as soon as they start to creep in— keeping my mind busy and staying working helps a lot. I'm always in the zone, trying to create content and build my brand. Creating content and meditating is my therapy. For so long, I thought alcohol, weed, and pills would take the pain away, but it only made things worse in reality.

I couldn't see it then, but I can see now how God puts us through certain situations to prepare us for our blessings. One of my favorite stories in the Bible is the book of Job. God allowed Satan to afflict Job. During this trying time, Job lost everything. His livestock, servants, and ten of his children died. Job questioned God, but he remained faithful, so he was rewarded twice what he had lost in the end. In many ways, I feel like Job. I lost so many people close to me, and a lot of people lost hope in me, but no matter what I was going through, I still had faith that God would turn things around for me.

We are only human and some things we don't understand. But I learned to trust his process because it's always going to work out in the end. Whenever I'm feeling down or low, I remind myself where I came from. I have been down and out. Sometimes I think back and can't believe I made it out of that situation, both physically and mentally. Trials and tribulations build character. If I weren't strong enough to handle it, God wouldn't have put me through it. If I can make it through, you can too. Once it's all said and done, you'll look back on your past with a smile.

I learned I have full control over my life and destiny. Looking back, the road was rocky for me, but I didn't let that stop me.

AGAINST ALL ODDS

This book is my testimony. It's for anyone who is currently in a dark place and can't seem to find a way out. Just look at me; I did it—and in some cases still doing it—*Against All Odds*. I was lost, but in life, sometimes you have to slow down and pay attention to the signs. They'll be the pieces you need to put your own puzzle together.

To all the parents who lost a child to gun violence, may God continue to comfort you. To everyone reading this that's suffering from anxiety, depression, or PTSD, I just want you to know I see you. I want to encourage you to hold on because you're worth the fight. There's a saying, meditate don't medicate. I can tell you from experience that medicating or using drugs to handle your problems isn't the way. I used to think it was cool to pop pain pills to cope, but it was damaging my overall health. I used to hate seeing my mom on drugs, as irony would have it, I followed in her footsteps. I had to break the generational curse over my family. And I'm doing my best, even now, to stay committed to this plan. Somedays are easier than others, honestly. I realized I had fans who looked forward to my work each and every day. It's bigger than me at this point.

I highly recommend anyone who is suffering from any mental health issues to seek help. It's okay to talk to someone about what you're going through or how you're feeling inside. Even if you can't afford professional help, find someone who cares about you. Help can come in many forms.

We tend to keep things bottled up. I would tell myself I was strong enough, but in reality, life can be too much to handle at times. It wasn't easy for me to pour my heart out in this book, but I felt like it could help someone— someone who looks like me or comes from where I come from. I'm here for you, and even if we're different, pain is pain, and I hope I was able to help you in some way.

I always thought getting help for mental illness was for weak people, or it just wouldn't help. But the more I ignored it, the more I realized I needed to seek help. For the young black men going through mental illness but feel like it's not cool to seek help, put your pride aside and get the help you need.

To all my dream chasers out there, no matter what situation you're in, it's still possible for you to become what you want. Get a vision board, write down your goals, and live as if you already have it. You are the rose that grew from concrete. The concrete is your struggle. Your struggle is motivation. Rise above it to become the person you were born to be. You are here for a reason. You got this.

Even with that said, there will always be things that will remind us of the trials we've faced. But I want to encourage you all not to think "struggle" when those bumps come. I'm a work-in-progress, will always be. I'm human. I still have my days, and life still presents challenges. This journey has taught me that with the challenges, it's important not to take the road of giving power to the struggle. That's it. That's the testimony, finding our power *through* our struggle.

ACKNOWLEDGMENTS

I would like to thank the people who helped me bring this book to life—first, my mom Lillian Wade and my dad William Green, who brought me into this world. I know our situation wasn't the best, but you did your best and I appreciate you giving me everything you could.

I want to thank my history teacher, Mr. Hill, for telling me if I didn't change the way I was acting, I would end up dead or in jail. Although I was only in the eighth grade, what you said resonated with me my whole life. Thank you! I want to thank Mr. Poindexter, my track coach in middle school, for being the first person to believe in me. You gave me hope, and I will never forget that.

To Richard Taylor Jr., my book coach, thank you for guiding me down the right path. The helpful information you gave me throughout the process was vital to making this book a success. I would also like to thank my editor,

Ashley M. King, "The Get It Done Queen," and her team for getting this book where it needed to be.

To Blair Caffey, thanks for seeing me. I'm grateful to have you in my life. I'm learning so much about the type of man I want to be by watching you.

To my big sis, Mia Francois (Auntie, when you're acting old, lol), thank you for believing in me and always being there for me and standing by me while we take my dreams to reality—including this book. I love you forever.

To my fans, I can't thank you enough for all the love. I appreciate every like, repost, comment, and share. I also want to send special love to everyone that ever DM'd me saying you were depressed or had thoughts of suicide, and my videos brought joy to your day. I don't take that lightly. I love you guys!

Thank you, Misha, Pops, and Marquis, for being my guardian angels. Not one day goes by I don't think of you guys. You are my motivation for everything I do. This book is for y'all. P.S., Marquis, we did it!

Last but not least, thank you, God. If I had a thousand tongues, I couldn't thank you enough.

ABOUT THE AUTHOR

Terrell Green is a social media comedian known for his famous reaction videos. He currently has over a quarter-million followers on Instagram tuning in daily for laughs. He lives in Fresno, California and loves to encourage young people to dream big no matter their circumstances. Terrell is excited to share his first book with you.

Instagram: @terrell_green
Facebook: Terrell Green
Twitter: @terrell__green
Website: www.terrellgreen.com

Manufactured by Amazon.ca
Bolton, ON

30812044R00035